CW00428895

BABY
SPICE
IN MY POCKET

EMMA

BOXTREE

First published in the UK in 1997 by Boxtree,
an imprint of Macmillan Publishers Ltd, 25 Eccleston Place, London,
SW1W 9NF and Basingstoke

Associated companies throughout the world

ISBN 0 7522 1157 9

Photographs: All Action – front & back cover,1, 4, 6, 9, 11, 13, 14, 17, 18,
22, 27, 32 & 33, 39, 44 & 45 Capital Pictures – 6, 21, 24 & 25, 31, 34, 36,
40, 43, 47, 48 Retna – endpapers, 3, 28

9 8 7 6 5 4 3 2 1

A CIP catalogue record for this book is available from the
British Library

Design by Blackjacks

Concept by Clare Hulton

Printed in Singapore

Neither the members of the Spice Girls nor any of their representatives
have had any involvement with this book.

Full name: Emma Lee Bunton

Date of birth: 21 January 1976

**Distinguishing marks:
A scar on her left knee**

Height: 5ft 2in

'DO I THINK MARGARET THATCHER IS THE ORIGINAL SPICE GIRL? NOT PARTICULARLY. MY MUM IS'

IN THE 'SAY YOU'LL BE THERE' VIDEO EMMA'S CHARACTER IS CALLED KUNG FU CANDY

EMMA IS PRINCE WILLIAM'S FAVOURITE SPICE GIRL

BABY SPICE'S MOTTO IS: 'BE SWEET, BE GOOD AND HONEST - ALWAYS.'

WHEN EMMA SMILED AT ULRIKA JONSSON AT THE BRIT AWARDS, ULRIKA DIDN'T SMILE BACK. SO NEXT TIME THEY MET EMMA PINCHED HER BUM!

EMMA COMES FROM FINCHLEY IN NORTH LONDON. SHE STARTED HER CAREER AT THE AGE OF FIVE AS A MODEL IN A MOTHERCARE CATALOGUE

BABY SPICE WOULD LOVE TO BE LENNY KRAVITZ'S ROCK CHICK

WHAT WOULD EMMA BE DOING IF SHE WEREN'T A SPICE GIRL? SHE'D BE FULFILLING HER OTHER AMBITION - TO WORK IN A SHOP

EMMA ONCE APPEARED IN AN EPISODE OF 'THE BILL' AND WOULD LIKE TO BE ABLE TO EAT 100 DOUGHNUTS IN TEN MINUTES

BABY SPICE FIRMLY BELIEVES THAT A GIRL'S BEST FRIEND IS HER MUM

EMMA ONCE AUDITIONED FOR THE PART OF BIANCA IN 'EASTENDERS'

EMMA'S TALENT IS HER HIGH VOICE – SHE DOES ALL THE HIGH LICKS. SHE'S ALSO VERY CARING AND IF ANYONE'S UNHAPPY SHE'LL TRY TO SORT IT OUT

EMMA STILL GETS GOOSE BUMPS WHEN SHE HEARS ONE OF THE SPICE GIRLS' SONGS

BABY SPICE FIRST APPEARED ON STAGE WHEN SHE WAS THREE. SHE CAN STILL REMEMBER WHAT IT WAS LIKE PLAYING THE SWAN WITH ALL THE OTHERS DANCING AROUND HER

VICTORIA SAYS THAT BABY SPICE IS THE LOVELIEST, CRAZIEST, FUNNIEST GIRL TO HAVE AROUND

EMMA HAS A HUGE COLLECTION OF SMELLY SOAPS

DON'T MESS WITH
BABY SPICE — SHE
HAS A BLUE BELT IN
KARATE AND HER
MUM, PAULINE, IS A
KARATE TEACHER

EMMA WAS A BIG TAKE THAT FAN — SHE HAD A MAD CRUSH ON MARK OWEN

BABY SPICE HAS A REPUTATION FOR BEING GRUMPY IN THE MORNINGS

AT A PARTY IN PORTUGAL, EMMA ASKED MULTI-MILLIONAIRE RICHARD BRANSON FOR A LIFT HOME IN HIS PRIVATE JET SO SHE COULD SEE HER MUM – HE SAID YES!